Acknowledgements

My thanks to all the staff at Tigh Filí but particularly to Nick Sanquest.
Thanks to Leo Ryan, Ian Wild and Breda Foran.
Special thanks to Michael McAnthony, Patricia Lyons,
Nadine Letort and Pleuni Kramer.
And, to Maire Bradshaw and Liz Willows.
I dedicate this book to all the children who sent in poems and illustrations,
this is only the beginning!

supported by

EUROCHILD 2000

EDITED BY AISLING LYONS

bradshaw books
Cork, Ireland

First published in 2000 by

bradshaw books
Tigh Filí (Poets' House)
Thompson House
MacCurtain Street
Cork, Ireland
Phone (353) 21 509274
Fax (353) 21 551617
Website www.tighfili.com

All rights reserved. No part of this book may be reprinted or reproduced or utilised in any electronic, mechanical, or other means, now known or hereafter invented, including photocopying and recording or otherwise, without prior written permission of the publishers or a licence permitting restricted copying in Ireland issued by the Irish Copyright Agency Ltd., the Irish Writers' Centre, 19 Parnell Square, Dublin 1.

British Library Cataloguing in Publication Data

ISBN 0 949010 69 3

Front cover collage by Eve O'Toole, Scoil Bhríde, Eglantine, Cork
Background sketch by Samantha Giles, Drumachose NS, Co. Londonderry
Cover design by Nick Sanquest
Typeset and layout at Tigh Filí
Printed and bound by Techman, Dublin

FOREWORD

It is with great pleasure that I write this foreword to Eurochild 2000 and pay tribute to the dedication of all those involved in its publication.

The German philosopher G.W.F. Hegel once described poetry as 'the universal art of the spirit that launches out exclusively in the inner space and inner time of ideas and feelings'. We find in Eurochild 2000 a concrete manifestation of that universal art, as the children of Europe explore their own inner worlds. In doing so they provide us with a fresh and delightful vision that we as adults are prone to have lost.

Writing is not a natural form of self-expression for children and they need encouragement in order to enhance their confidence in using it as a means of communication. A project like Eurochild 2000 encourages and enhances the confidence of the children involved. It also embodies many of the concepts that national curricula propose as learning objectives. Teachers throughout Europe can use this publication as a resource for encouraging their own pupils to explore their inner time and inner space of ideas and feelings.

I congratulate warmly the Cork Womens Poetry Circle and everyone who has been involved in the project.

Dr Michael Woods
Minister for Education and Science

INTRODUCTION

L'an 2000 voit paraître la sixième édition d'Eurochild. Ce partenariat Eurochild - Euro Ecole a tenu ses promesses. Grâce au dévouement des uns et des autres, il a pu se concrétiser dans la durée, en apportant à chaque édition une collaboration toujours meilleure pour une qualité grandissante.

Mais Eurochild n'existerait pas sans les enfants. L'abondance des productions montre leur besoin de s'exprimer, leur intérêt pour la création poétique. Grâce à Eurochild, leurs poèmes sont imprimés dans un «vrai» livre, et lus dans l'Europe entière. Les enfants sont respectés, reconnus comme poètes, quels que soit leur langue, leur âge, leur niveau social ou culturel. Ce n'est plus l'apanage des «grands». Les reconnaître aujourd'hui, c'est leur donner confiance pour demain, pour bâtir un avenir qui, par la poésie, restera vigilant au respect des droits de l'homme et à la liberté d'expression.

J'espère de tout coeur qu'Eurochild se prolonge pendant de nombreuses années et je remercie tous ceux qui oeuvrent pour faire de ce projet commun une réussite.

Isabelle Brondy
Présidente d'Euro Ecole

CONTENTS

HAPPY TO BE

Journey to Dreamland	Eibhlís Ní Fhearchaillaigh	3
How they Danced	Laura Cassin	4
My Favourite Chair	Caoimhe Mahony	5
Peace	Joan Barber	6
Ice-skater	Annie Lawrence	6
The Sun	Reggie Sweetnam	7
Happy Poem	Caitlin Dagg	7

CREEP, CROUCH, POUNCE

My Little Fish	Emma Counihan	11
The Little Tiny Bird	Jack Walsh	11
The Horse that God Forgot	Jonathan Pearson	12
De Kikker	Benjamin Tol	13
My Wish	Peter Devlin	13
Les Animaux du Zoo	Melanie Boutteau	14
Silent Flight	Maurice Hamilton	15
My Little Black Cat	Stephanie Madden	16
Crocodiles	Aisling Fitzgerald	17
Noise	Ruth Vaughan	18
Dogs	Rachel Dooey	19
My Dog's Reaction	Cara Sanquest	20
My Little Tadpole	Harry Porter	20
Brown Bear	Camille Hurley	21
Frog	Adrian Doyle	22
The Bee	Max Bartolo	23
The Fish	Gillian O'Connell	23
Free	Athena Corcoran-Tadd	24
My Fish Sam	Gemma McAlary	24
Les Oiseaux	Amélie Guichard	25
Barn Owl	Richard Bowers	26
Fudge	Sîan Barry	26
De Koe	Jan de Dood	27
Girouette	Stéphanie Duguay	27
Licorne	Thomas Lauriane	27
De Goudvis	Wouter van Tongeren	28

Les Chevaux	Orjang Dycke	29
The Little Bird	Damian Cilia	30
My Cat	Aleisha Moore	31
My Little Doggy	Kelly Forde	31
My Fish	Christina Columb	32
Huskies	Benjamin Dagg	33
De Leeuw	Tristan Gider	34
Squeaky	Janet Berka	34
Cats	Aileen O'Mahony	35
The Bad Rat	Aimee O'Driscoll	35
Slithery Sandy the Snake	Micha Healy	36
Les Animaux	Kristell Houël	37

THE HARD TRACK

Good-bye	Kate Martin	41
Bullies	Christine McKimm	42
Statue	Moll Linehan	42
Before it's too Late	Aoife McKenna	43
A Viking Village	Ruth Corscadden	44
The Voice	Sheila McSweeney	45
The Hedge School	Andrea McGoey	46
Hidden from Sight	Simon Anthony Ley	47
The Old Narrow Track	Cora Savage	48
Klaus hat ein Haus	Kathrin Elskemper	48

YELLOW BANANAS

Yellow Bananas	Karen Poynton	51
The Rainbow	Jessica van der Puil	51
L'Arc-En-Ciel	Marion Bernard	52
The Song of the Sea	Síle Ní Úrdail	53
Big Wave	Aoife Gorman	54
Hello	Ciara Ní Lionnáin	55
Mr Moon	Athena Corcoran-Tadd	56
The Woods	Labhrás Ó'Conchúir	57
Snowflake	Julian Hemphill	58
The Sun	Diarmuid O'Mahony	58
La Vie sous la Mer	Marion Varganyi	59
The Bog	Sophie Dalton	60

The Blue	Eibhlís Ní Fhearchaillaigh	61
By the Sands	Sarah Robb	62
Ice	Gemma Pudney	63
Ice	Jade Turner	63
The Sea	Eibhlís Ní Fhearchaillaigh	64
Ocean	Andrew Hobbs	65
La Tempête	Charlotte Mahé	66
The Wind	Sarah Pearson	67
Lightning	Hannah Dimond	68
Why was I not Told?	Breffney Cogan	68
Les Tornades	David Mouraud	69
La Marée Noire	Damien Trochu	70
It's Raining	Zita McCarthy	71
Leaves	Colm Ó'Drisceoil	72
Far Away	Shannen McKeegan	72
The Tree	Dawn Thompson	72

A MAGIC GARDEN

The Monster I Met	Sharon Ruane	75
The Alien Hair Grabber	Rebecca Noonan	76
Our Journey	Andrea McGoey	77
The Magic Garden	Kevin Collins	78
Venus	Jessica Mullins	79
Ene Mene	Kathrin Elskemper	79
Humpty Dumpty	Conor Higgins	79
Muumio	Nadia Kähkönen & Noora Hannula	80
Clematis Faction	Joe Hughes	81
The Onion Head	Maitiú MacArdáil	82
The Multifever	Andrew Waugh	83
Superboy	James O'Mahony	84
I had a Dream	Andrew Duignan	85
Venus Sneezed	Moll Linehan	86
My Throat	Moll Linehan	86
Papa Passe la Paille	Camille Duval	87
The Silly Family	Raphael Buttigieg	87
Hippopotemela	Ruth Vaughan	88
Alienation	Joe Hughes	89
De UFO	Wouter Ekelaar	90

One Bright Morning	Labhrás Ó'Conchúir	91
The Silvery Woods	Orla Thompson	92
Father Time	Christine O'Mahony	93
Headus	Jerl Norden	94
L'Ange et le Citron	Ewen Qellec	94
My Balloon	Niamh Jordan	95

THE LEAVES ARE TURNING

Seasons	Deborah Donnelly	99
Autumn	Niall Ó'Dulacháin	100
Autumn	Aileen O'Mahony	100
Autumn Time	Carly McClenaghan	101
Autumn	Shane Redmond	102
Winter	Andrew Hobbs	103
L'Hiver	Heloïse Moune	104
Winter	Aidin Hegarty	105
A Winter's Morn	Conchúr Ó'Tréinfhir	105
Awakening	Jonathan Morrow	106
Spring	Shane O'Sullivan	107
Spring	Kate Murphy	108

CELEBRATE

Easter	Maitiú MacArdáil	111
Hallowe'en	Shane Redmond	112
Hallowe'en Pie	Jim O'Hagan	113
The Life of Witches	Jean-Pierre Pace	114
An Sciathán Leathair	Diarmaid De Bhál	115
The Haunted Woods	Daniel Manning	116
Walking Alone in the Dark	Claudio Caruana	117
Hallowe'en	Christine O'Mahony	118
Haunted House	Gerard Black	119
The Ghost	Jane Quinn	120
A Scare	Aimée Auchincloss	121
Christmas Time	Ailbhe Cashman	122
A Christmas Eve	Anniina Koskinen	123
Oíche Nollag	Lianne Ní Chárthaigh	124
Joulukuusi	Katriina Hallama & Onerva Heikka	125

Fireworks	Colm Ó'Drisceoil	125
The Special Star	Jane Moriarty	126
L'An 2000	Anaïs Tuco	127
Midnight 2000	Brian Heappey	128
Pour l'An 2000	Marie Bellugue	129
A l'An 2000	Haili-Michaël	130
Millennium Feelings	Vanessa Meade	131

NINE INNINGS

In the Park	Mark Camilleri	135
La Musique	Teerapong Dabreteau	136
Tooth Fairy	Linda Kelly	136
Teacher Fell into the Pool	James O'Mahony	137
C'est Bien	Arthur Templé	137
La Maîtresse	Cindy Garda	138
Mammy	Patrick Cronin	138
The Beach	Ailbhe Cashman	139
Pourquoi?	Arnaud le Cadre	139
A Street Full of Noisy Traffic	Jean-Pierre Pace	140
Suomi	Taru Takamaa	141
Little Boys	Clodagh Hogan	142
Soccer	Stephen Field	143
Spiderman	Edward O'Rourke	144
I Don't Mind	Catherine Hayes	145
A Visit to the Doctor	Doireann Ní Ghráinne	146
The Playground	Sophie Kearney	147
Suomen Luonto	Nadia Kähkönen	147
Poème	Servane Warot	148
De Toekomst	Assia Khetib	149
La Belgique	Mickaël	149
Candles	Jenny Gough	150
I have a Dream	David Fitzgerald	152
A Dream	Siobhán Coady	153
My Dream	Aoife Corcoran	154
Les Mitaines	Chloé Mitaine	155
La Belgique	Aline et Amandine	156
The Swing	Amy Nutt	156

LOVE REIGNS

The Snowman	Rachel McDonald	159
Not Gone	Ailbhe Cashman	160
Love	Denis Murphy	161
Colm	James Hayes	162
James	Colm Buckley	163
Love Reigns	Maurice Hamilton	164
We are in Love	Eamonn Mulholland	165
Max	Ashley Henderson	166
Human Rainbow	Cara Sanquest	166
Lahkus	Mirjam Pilv	167
Headus	Mirjam Pilv	167
Soprus	Mirjam Pilv	167
Erinnerung	Désirée Scheer	168

IN DARKNESS LIGHT

Coffins	Leslie Spillane	171
Stuck	Rebecca Noonan	172
Death	Michael Hurley	173
The Wave	Patricia Prunty	174
The Wall	Eilis McGleur	175
Heaven	Simeon Lenz-Lipitch	176
Les Maladies Graves	Marion Colas	177
There was an Old Man	Astrid Coughlan	178
Guns of Sorrow	Jessica Lynch	179
The Haunting	Stephanie Fleming	180
To a Strange Place	Jill Collins	181
Grandad	Sarah Bowe	182
Ich Sah Sie!	Désirée Scheer	183
Missbraucht und Weggeworfen	Désirée Scheer	184
The Old Priest	Ciara Egan	185

ILLUSTRATIONS

Front cover collage by Eve O'Toole, Scoil Bhríde, Eglantine, Cork
Background sketch by Samantha Giles, Drumachose NS, Co. Londonderry

Coughlan, Astrid	Rockboro NS, Cork	7
Columb, Christina	St Joseph's, Longford	10-11
Hart, Emma	Rockboro NS, Cork	16
Dagg, Benjamin	Innishannon, Co. Cork	19
Cotter, Josh	Rockboro NS, Cork	21
Hart, Emma	Rockboro NS, Cork	22
O'Toole, Evan	Rockboro NS, Cork	25
Coughlan, Astrid	Rockboro NS, Cork	30
Broecker, Katie	Rockboro NS, Cork	31
Barry, Niamh	Creative Writing Class, Cork	41
Corcoran-Tadd, Fionn	Ballydehob, Co. Cork	45
Lawrence, Nancy	St Joseph's, Longford	46
O'Dwyer, Chloe	Scoil Bhríde, Eglantine, Cork	56
Linehan, Moll	Creative Writing Class, Cork	59
Kirke, Robert	Drumachose NS, Co. Londonderry	64
Bushe-Murphy, Billie	Rockboro NS, Cork	66-67
Miller, Jayne		76
Corcoran-Tadd, Athena	Ballydehob, Co. Cork	78
Kelleher, Jessica	Creative Writing Class, Cork	83
Bardon, Paul	Creative Writing Class, Cork	84
Cotter, Josh	Rockboro NS, Cork	85
Bardon, Paul	Creative Writing Class, Cork	88
Cotter, Josh	Rockboro NS, Cork	90
Nevin, Christine	St Joseph's, Longford	92
Shiels, Laura	Drumachose NS, Co. Londonderry	102
Conway, Caroline	Nenagh, Co. Tipperary	108
El Sayed, Adham	Rockboro NS, Cork	113
Pace, Jean-Pierre	Stella Maris College, Malta	114
Kelleher, Jessica	Creative Writing Class, Cork	117
O'Neill, Julie	Rockboro NS, Cork	122
McCarthy, Rebecca	Rockboro NS, Cork	127
Lawrence, Annie	St Joseph's, Longford	128-129
Cotter, Josh	Rockboro NS, Cork	130
Pace, Jean-Pierre	Stella Maris, Malta	140-141

Hemphill, Julian	Drumachose NS, Co. Londonderry	143
Paul, Lia	Creative Writing Class, Cork	145
Gough, Jenny	Scoil Bhríde, Eglantine, Cork	151
Porter, Harry	St Luke's, Cork	160
O'Toole, Eve	Scoil Bhríde, Eglantine, Cork	165
Porter, Harry	St Luke's, Cork	166
McCarthy, Rebecca	Rockboro NS, Cork	176
Coughlan, Astrid	Rockboro NS, Cork	178

Happy
To
Be

EIBHLÍS NÍ FHEARCHAILLAIGH

Journey to Dreamland

Silence, listen to the rain
Silence, against the windowpane

Feel the warmth, beneath the sheet
Storm clouds outside look like black sheep

Think about them in your mind
And very soon you will find

That these sights and sounds when mixed together
Accompanied by a pillow of feather

Can help you relax and slip away
Into your dreamland and there you will stay.

Laura Cassin

How they Danced

How they danced on a cold cold day,
How her hair blew in every way.
The way he twirled her,
Her dress shone bright
Oh how the audience cheered with delight.

She jumped and twirled
Her long golden hair sparkled and whirled.
As she smiled and bowed
To the big happy crowd
The crowd clapped aloud.

Caoimhe Mahony

My Favourite Chair

I sit over there in my chair, not only to stare out the window
I sit on my chair, my purple and green checked chair with
Four blue ribbons on each mahogany leg.
It's old, battered and bruised
I don't care because it's my lovely, comfortable, purple chair.

I miss my chair when I go to school but when I come home
I shout, 'Yahoo!'
'It's homework time,' I say
Some people think I'm crazy
But I don't care because I get to sit in my comfortable chair.

I sit on my chair till my homework is done and my mum tells me to
Go out and play
I always do prefer rainy days so my mum can't tell me to go out and play
I will sit in front of our big TV in my
purple and green checked chair with
Blue ribbons on each mahogany leg.

Joan Barber

Peace

As the leaves fall
gently into the sea
and the foam quietly breaks
on the craggy rocks
the water swishes
onto the soft quiet sand.
I can feel the peace.

Annie Lawrence

Ice-skater

The ice-skater looks
So light and graceful
As she glides across
The frozen lake
She swirls and twirls
In a world of her own
She guides her smiles
Happy to be free
To dance
To be.

Reggie Sweetnam

The Sun

The Sun is shining
Everyone is smiling
What a happy day.

Caitlin Dagg

Happy Poem

Wind, wind, wind is blowing.
I am happy.

Creep Crouch Pounce

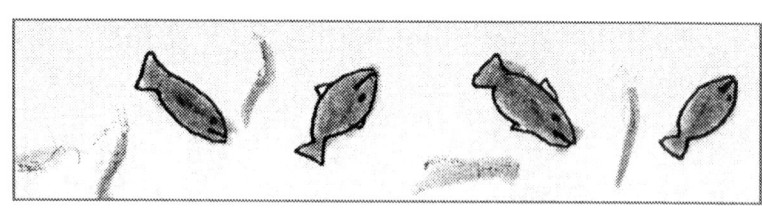

Emma Counihan

My Little Fish

I had a little fish
I put it on my dish
He wriggled and giggled
He stayed alive
But then he sighed
And then he died.

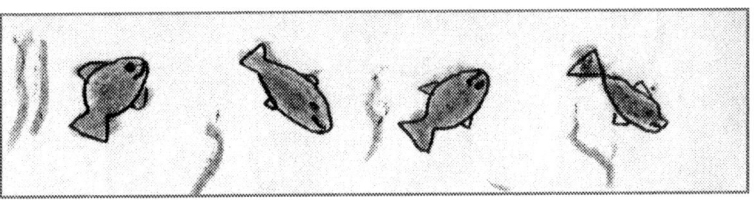

Jack Walsh

The Little Tiny Bird

There was a little tiny bird
who said he was fantastic
He said he was going to make a nest
from twigs and black elastic

He made it on a big fat branch
that wasn't very steady
Then one day the branch fell down
before the nest was ready.

JONATHAN PEARSON

The Horse that God Forgot

As the rugged pony looked upon
The new white stallion, swift and strong,
As he saw his master, his heart sank
And he turned his head to the nearby bank.

His coat wasn't shiny or neat
That young white stallion, impossible to beat...
His bloodshot eyes, his crying face
He knew he was an utter disgrace

His rusty fur, his skinny bones
He was as weak as a newborn foal
Frustration hanging on his face
He finally lost his guilty case

As he lay down to eternal rest
Remembering he used to be the best
He didn't achieve much, not a lot
That poor old horse that God forgot.

BENJAMIN TOL

De Kikker

Hij springt, hij spat over het water
Maar een dagje later gaat hij onder water
Daar gaat hij eten halen
Waterspinnen zijn favoriet
Maar als hij een lekker vliegje ziet
Dan weigert hij niet hem te pakken
Of bij een vliegje onder water te zakken.
Daar zal hij gerust veel moeite voor doen.
Want als hij niet goed kan eten
Kan hij z'n leven wel vergeten.

PETER DEVLIN

My Wish

I wish I had a lion
I'd take him into school
Then teacher wouldn't scold me
If I broke any rule
He'd sit down right beside me
Growl at all the girls and boys
And when it came to playtime
I'd have the pick of all the toys.

Mélanie Boutteau

Les Animaux du Zoo

Au zoo aujourd'hui
Il y a du bruit:
Les singes font des acrobaties
La hyène rit
Le castor aussi.

Les lions rugissent
Devant Maurice
Le distribueur de viandes
Non friandes.

Le zèbre décampe
Car les hippocampes
L'envoient en exil
Paraît-il.

Le serpent tremblotte
Et la marmotte
Met ses bottes
Rigolottes.

Tout ça en une journée
Si vous les suivez
Vous verrez,
Vous vous amuserez.

Maurice Hamilton

Silent Flight

The sun was setting
Behind a hill
When the hoot of an owl
Made everything still

Its mysterious eyes
Combed the ground
Its silent flight
Made no sound

Its feathers muffled
The sound of its wings
While it hunted for mice
And other nice things

Its eyes are keen
It's often heard
Seldom seen
A nocturnal bird.

Stephanie Madden

My Little Black Cat

Across the floor as sly as a fox
Comes my little black cat out of her box
She moves smoothly and with grace
When all of a sudden my dog gives chase.
My little black cat taken to her paws
My little black cat uncovers her claws
With one move she scratches his nose
My dog gives a big yelp!
Then I realise my little black cat doesn't need any help
My big bold dog is put out of the house
My little black cat is quiet as a mouse
Her uncovered claws go back into place
Because now she knows she has won the chase.

AISLING FITZGERALD

Crocodiles

Crocodiles have toothy smiles
If you have sense you'll run a mile
They are wicked, cunning and sly
And they think as they look at you, 'Mmm, human pie!'

They gaze at you with greedy eyes
And throw at you a bunch of lies
'How are you dear? You're looking thinner,'
But really saying, 'Here comes dinner.'

You're looking at the riverbank
And everything is still
Until you see that swishing tail
They're ready for the kill

That fishy grin, those countless teeth
It's really you they want to eat
When you get close, without a sound
They have you down upon the ground

I hope that message has got through
Because that's what is behind you – BOO!

Ruth Vaughan

Noise

A dog barked at a cat
Who pitter-pattered after a chick
Who hid behind its squawking mother
Who with a rustle of her feathers
And a quick swish of her tail
Warned a yelping cat to stay away
So…

The yelping cat skidded straight into a clattering bucket
Which fell on a chirping chick
Who called its clucking mother to the rescue
Who after many fruitless attempts
Discovered that clattering buckets
Won't get off chirping chicks for squawking mothers
So…

She sat on a squeaky gate to think aloud
Before falling into a field of squelchy…
Muck?
She then started clucking, squawking and squelching
All at the same time
Which…

Worried the whistling farmer's wife
Who came plodding to the rescue
And, when she found a barking dog, a yelping cat, a chirp-
ing chick
(under a clattering bucket)
And a clucking, squawking, squelching hen
She…
Put socks in all of their mouths!

Rachel Dooey

Dogs

Dogs run jump sleep in
Kennels chairs anywhere anyplace
They like to talk to one another
Their coats blow in the wind
Some like to fight
Each other at night
They howl and bark
When morning comes
They scratch the doorway
They like to lick your face
When night comes
They bark
All night long.

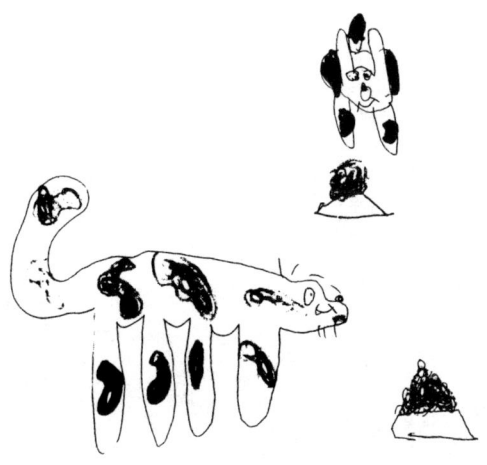

CARA SANQUEST

My Dog's Reaction

On my eighth birthday I got a kitten
I already had a dog so cute and cuddly
When I came home with my new kitten
My dog was surprised, he sniffed his bum and
Wagged his tail, it really was quite funny
My dog was very jealous
For the next four or five weeks
You could not go near the cat or the dog
In the end they both made friends
And here I am now
With my dog sitting on my bed
Writing my poem
At five past ten
All on my own
With my dog.

HARRY PORTER

My Little Tadpole

Underneath the waterweeds
Small and black I wriggle
All my life is most surprising
Wriggle, wraggle, wriggle.

CAMILLE HURLEY

Brown Bear

There was a brown bear
Who sat on a chair
Brushing and brushing his hair so straight
Because he was going on a date.

Adrian Doyle

Frog

Once there was a frog named Tim
His problem was he couldn't swim
He went to see the Wizard Drake
The Wizard Drake lived in a lake

He hopped and hopped to see the Wizard
But on the way there was a blizzard
It got him there in a hurry
And then the Drake said to scurry

He pulled the frog into his nest
And asked, 'What's your problem, can I help?'
He gave the frog the magic spell
And then the frog hopped off to hell.

Max Bartolo

The Bee

The bee is so yellow
As nice as can be
He's such a good fellow
Making honey for me

Loving and sharing
Doing what's right
Always during the day
But never at night

Though at night
He does sleep
Dreaming of honey
Ever so sweet.

Gillian O'Connell

The Fish

Little slimy fish
Its colours are so lovely
Oh what a nice fish.

ATHENA CORCORAN-TADD

Free

A dolphin swims through the sea
looking for fish to have for tea.
Ah, there's a fish
he does not need
To make a fish dish out of greed.
He doesn't have to wash a plate.
He can always stay up late!

He likes to swim
he likes to leap
he comes up from the murky deep.
He leaps up high into the air
then goes diving down
without a care.

GEMMA McALARY

My Fish Sam

Round and round
Up and down
That's all I do all day
I wish I could get out of here
Go somewhere else to play.

Amélie Guichard

Les Oiseaux

Les oiseaux dans le ciel
ont de belles ailes couleur miel.
Ils volent dans les airs
aussi légers que les blés verts.
Les oiseaux voleurs le bec dans la corbeille
volent la groseille rouge vermeille.
Les oiseaux se baignent dans l'eau couleur du ciel
et suivent les abeilles.

Richard Bowers

Barn Owl

White feathers with a little brown
Dark, wide eyes to look around
Comes out at night
To find his prey
You won't see him through the day
A little mouse may come his way
The owl may swoop and
Carry him away.

Sîan Barry

Fudge

I had a bird
I called him Fudge
I put him in a cage
And now he won't budge

My cat is going crazy
He's usually quite lazy
His parents are circling above
But Fudge sticks like a glove

Soon he'll be gone
Like the wind in a song
I will miss him.

Jan de Dood

De Koe

De koe zegt boe
en hij is vaak moe
hij heeft vier magen
en daarvoor hoef je hem echt niet te plagen.

Stéphanie Duguay

Girouette

Oh Girouette
Ma petite ponette
Quand je te vois galoper
J'ai envie de te monter
Avec tes yeux couleur d'ébène
Tu ressembles à une petite reine
Dans mon coeur tu es entrée
A jamais je ne pourrai t'oublier.

Thomas Lauriane

Licorne

Les licornes battent leur record
Mais elles galopent si loin
Qu'elles perdent leur corne conique
Et clic!

Wouter van Tongeren

De Goudvis

De vis, de vis, de gouden vis
Hij zwemt door de sloten van zwabberish
Aan de oever staat de ooievaar
met stekeltjeshaar
De vis denkt, 'Wat is dat voor een gek
Met zijn lange bek?'
De ooievaar vliegt weg
Het gevaar is geweken
maar over drie weken
Zal hij bezwijken
Hij heeft niet lang meer te leven
De vis trilt van het beven
Want hij vreest voor zijn leven.

ORJANG DYCKE

Les Chevaux

Les chevaux sont de toutes les couleurs;
Blancs, noirs, marron, bais, café au lait...
On ne sait pas vraiment combien il y en a.
Ils peuvent courir pendant les heures;
Ça s'appelle galoper, je crois.
Monter à cru, en selle
Dans les bois, le soir
A la mer, un soir de Noël
Plutôt que de les laisser choir
Dans leurs boxes ou dans leurs prés
Tous seuls, abandonnés
Qui ne voudrait pas d'un cheval aux reflets roux?
Pourtant, si je ne me trompe pas,
Les chevaux naissent, aiment, vieillissent et meurent comme nous
Pourquoi les traitons-nous comme des esclaves?
Ils ont des yeux, des oreilles, une bouche, des jambes,
des 'cheveux', un dos, des poumons et un coeur,
Comme nous.

Damian Cilia

The Little Bird

The little bird all red and white
I love with all my heart
It sings with all its might
And it fills my heart.

It flies here and there
But it doesn't go away
Its song fills the air
All through the day.

At night it comes to rest
In a tree full of leaves
Home in its comfortable nest
Anything behind it leaves.

Aleisha Moore

My Cat

Creep
Crouch
Pounce
Snatch
Lucky's up to her tricks again

Kelly Forde

My Little Doggy

My little doggy has sharp, sharp teeth
They come out of his mouth almost touching his feet
When he puts up a fight with the poodle next door
He'll stick in his teeth and
Won't be bothered no more.

CHRISTINA COLUMB

My Fish

I had a little fish
When I was very small
I used to pick him up
My mum said 'Don't let him fall.
Put him in his tank, it's where
He likes to be.'
I put him in the water
But he began to falter,
He was not very well.
He fell
To the bottom
And floated to the top,
Sadly my little fish had died
I cried
And cried
And cried.

Benjamin Dagg

Huskies

Huskies white
Huskies brown
Huskies dapple grey,
Huskies weak
Huskies strong
Help to pull the sleigh.

Huskies have
Amber eyes
That glitter like the sun,
Huskies play
All the day
When their work is done.

Tristan Gider

De Leeuw

De leeuw jaagt in de avond
de leeuw jaagt in de nacht
dan ligt hij stilletjes op de grond
als hij een prooi verwacht

Dan ziet hij een ree, hij springt, hij doodt!
met een slag van zijn enorme poot
dan is het weer stil
het gras geeft een ruis
hij sleurt het ree mee naar huis.

Janet Berka

Squeaky

My hamster is the cutest thing
He's small and brown and fuzzy
He sleeps all day and then we play
Ohh! He's on my tummy!

Aileen O' Mahony

Cats

I like cats
Big cats
Small cats
Fat cats
Thin cats
Noisy cats
Quiet cats
Sleepy cats
Playful cats
My black cat
Comes when I call
Cats! Cats!
I like them all.

Aimee O'Driscoll

The Bad Rat

You rat, you rat
You little bad rat
You frightened my cat
And if you frighten my cat again
You will be a dead rat.

Micha Healy

Slithery Sandy the Snake

Down came a snake from a tree
Sliding, slithering, down the tree
She said her name was Sandy
She wrapped herself around me
She tried to strangle me
But she was very slithery and so she slipped off me.

She thought that she was cool
But I thought that she was cruel
Sandy slithered up the tree
While I ran home not knowing I had
Forgotten my key
Sandy Snake changed her mind and decided to slither after me
So I ran and ran as fast as I still can.

She looked at me as if I was as small as a bee
But she still slithered and slithered after me
My mom was at home, she answered the door quickly
Because she knew that I was alone
Sandy Snake still lives in the tree and
She did not get to eat me.

KRISTELL HOUËL

Les Animaux

Là-haut sur la colline
Il y a une lapine
Elle a l'air très coquine
Mais aussi très maligne
Elle s'appelle Eglantine.

Là-haut sur le Mont-Blanc
Il y a un élan
Il n'a pas l'air méchant
Mais il est quand même inquiétant
Ça doit être une maman.

Là-bas sur le terrain
Il y a un gros chien
Il n'a pas l'air bien
Mais sans doute il n'a rien
Il s'appelle Sébastien.

The Hard Track

KATE MARTIN

Good-bye

We played and laughed
We always joked about,
But when my best friend moved away
My candle was blown out.

We used to meet on Saturdays
See movies, chat and shop,
But when my best friend moved away
The fun and laughter stopped.

We used to sit together in school
Always side by side,
But when my best friend moved away
It felt like someone died.

Christine McKimm

Bullies

I stood lonely as a cloud
I was not feeling proud
They were very loud

I would say, 'Hi, can I play?'
They would say, 'Go away.'
I tried not to cry
But I couldn't help myself.

Moll Linehan

Statue

Cold and lonely standing still
Trapped inside a stony skin
Up upon a pedestal
Watching a drunk man drink
He can't see his ankles where
One thousand names are there
People come and ooh and aah
And say what a beautiful thing
But only he knows the pain
Of standing, alone and still
Birds come and nest on him
Pecking out his hair.

Aoife McKenna

Before it's too Late

The landscape cries
For a new dawn
When sheep give lamb and
Deer give fawn

In all the land
Not a leaf to be found
There is no life
In what was ground

The soul of the sun
The life of the tree
They are all gone
Time to pay the fee

And though we deny it
It is all ruined now
Do not pretend
You don't know how

We've all played a part in this war
Let's stop now before it's too late
Never again
Will we mess with fate.

Ruth Corscadden

A Viking Village

Saddened, worried and excited families wave
As a longboat glides away
To unexplored lands
Not knowing when or if it will return.

Looking out along the silvery fjord
A longboat does return to welcoming friends
What treasures have they brought?
What stories have they to tell of foreign lands?

The village people gather together
Around a fire with a storyteller
He has brooches, jewels and other jewellery
To help bring life to his sagas

But life must return to normal
Seeds to sow, vegetables to gather
Corn to grind, water to carry
Life is hard for a little Viking.

Sheila McSweeney

The Voice

Answer the voice, give to the poor
To those who have been torn by war
Ripped of their dignity
Stripped of their rights
Who live in fear every night.
Not enough food
Not enough to drink
Death, they are on the brink
Do help the young
Do help the old
These people are very cold.
Answer the voice
Give to the poor
Until the world is finished with war.

ANDREA MCGOEY

The Hedge School

We come here to learn everyday
Without the English knowing.
But we go indoors in winter
When it is snowing.

They don't like us learning
They think it is a crime
So we have someone on guard
As lookout every time.

I'm going to be the lookout now
Lest they are on their way.
Please don't repeat
All that I did say.

Simon Anthony Ley

Hidden from Sight

I see her everyday, going on her way

She has a life she is so happy
I stand in a corner all by myself in a dream

I hide alone so no one can see such sadness
An empty soul wanting to die, I don't blame it

All I can do is think of her and try to be
Happy

I ask myself, 'Why her? Why me? Why?'
Why? Because she is she. Why me? Because
I am destined for
Pain

Along the highway of life, I just might maybe
Find a person who is going to be just right

Hopefully, Hell will come to an end…I pray

So cold
So dark
So dead.

CORA SAVAGE

The Old Narrow Track

As Bridget was walking down the old narrow track
She passed by a baker with bread in his sack
She put out a hand from under her cloak
And these are the words she softly spoke:
'Please give me a loaf for my sisters and me
and we'll share tonight as we sit at our tea.'
But the baker he muttered and shook a mean head,
'If you want to eat sister then bake your own bread'.
She looked in his eyes then, but all that she found
Was a star that was hard as the stones on the ground
So Bridget passed quietly along the hard track
As the bread turned to stone on the cold baker's back.

KATHRIN ELSKEMPER

Klaus hat ein Haus

Klaus hat ein Haus
da wirft ihn einer raus
Doch in diesem Haus
lebt auch eine Maus
Und die will nicht da raus
Klaus hat ein Haus
darin lebt eine Maus.

Yellow Bananas

Karen Poynton

Yellow Bananas

Stranded on the shore
The sea, restless
Against the golden sand,

The canoe nestling
Beneath the smooth slippy rocks,
The light fading.

I scan the trees
Blowing in the gentle breeze
For yellow bananas.

Jessica van der Puil

The Rainbow

The rainbow of fun
is there for everyone.
It shines rays of fun into you
and I'm not telling a story
this is true.
So, if you're sad at any time,
Just ask the rainbow to shine.

Marion Bernard

L'Arc-En-Ciel

Comme tu es beau,
Mon Arc-En-Ciel.
Avec tes sept couleurs
Marquées dans le ciel.

J'aimerais bien, moi
Venir te voir
Le soir
Quand il est tard.

Mais c'est impossible!
Tu es déjà couché
Et je ne veux pas te réveiller.

Demain matin,
Quand le Soleil sera levé,
Quand la pluie sera tombée,
Je prendrai mon manteau,
Et j'irai découvrir le Monde d'En Haut.

Je découvrirai beaucoup de Secrets
Dans ce monde si discret.

Mais comment ferai-je,
Pour monter dans le Monde d'En Haut?
C'est si haut…

Oh, l'Arc-En-Ciel
Fait des merveilles,
Il pourra me transporter
De bas en haut ou de haut en bas
En un claquement de doigts.

Vous pourrez venir avec moi le voir
Demain matin,
Mais je ne vous promets rien!

Síle Ní Úrdail

The Song of the Sea

I am the sea rolling along
The children are playing
I'm singing my song
Whoosh, whish, I sing

I'm massive, I'm huge
I'm as big as a giant
I roll in so fast the children
Think I'm a pirate
I'm blue, I'm deep
I'm a creep
And inside of me there's
A fish family tree

I'm the sea
So wild and free
The beautiful sea
That's me.

Aoife Gorman

Big Wave

As I prance up and down
Like horses in excitement
People running for their lives
I cover the land, the crops,
Everything that once was seen
And now is gone, vanished, disappeared.

I cover the houses
One by one
As people scream and hide
I fall back into the sea
and disappear.

As people return
They cry and wail
To see their houses
Destroyed by me
Big Wave.

Ciara Ní Lionnáin

Hello

The sun said, 'Hello'
to the rain and snow

'Hello,' said the clouds
as they passed the crowds

Daffodils bow
their pretty heads
'Hello,' they say
to the flower beds.

It is not hard
To say 'Hello'
A laugh and a smile
Will last a while.

Athena Corcoran-Tadd

Mr Moon

Mr Moon, with your silver face
that smiles as you pull the tide in
you shine in my window
I cannot sleep.
I look at you.
You are still smiling.
I ask quietly,
'Please Mr Moon
I cannot sleep for you are so bright.
Could you not shine so much?
Please?'
So, Mr Moon moves across the sky.
Slowly.

Labhrás Ó'Conchúir

The Woods

Tall trees
Small trees
Chopped trees
All sorts of trees

Green leaves
Brown leaves
Red leaves
Whispering breeze

Mushy ground
Dry ground
Leafy ground
No stones around

Sheltered and dark
Animals roam
Birds at home
This is the woods.

JULIAN HEMPHILL

Snowflake

Glittery, shining, frozen
Droplets of water
Falling gracefully like a
Ballet dancer turning
Landing on top of other snowflakes
To cover the fields with a
Blanket of snow.
That is a snowflake.

DIARMUID O'MAHONY

The Sun

The sun is bright
the sun is warm
It brings the dawn
in the morn

The sun can burn
the sun is bright
The sun is dangerous
but it goes down at night

The sun is big
the sun can tan
The sun is hotter
than a frying-pan.

Marion Varganyi

La Vie sous la Mer

En plongeant
J'ai vu!
Un piranha
Danser la salsa

Un dauphin et un requin
Jouer du tambourin

Un saumon
Faire des bonds

Une anguille
Jouer aux quilles

Une raie
Manger un brochet.

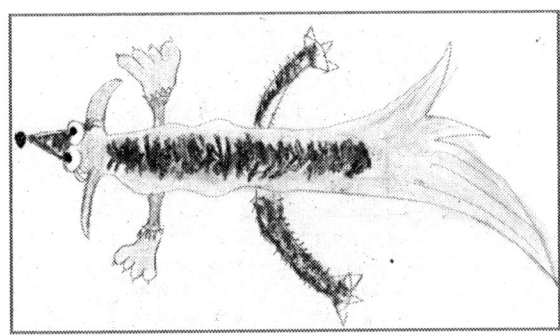

Sophie Dalton

The Bog

White bog cotton
Swaying in the wind
Beautiful purple heather
Dazzling in the sun
Tiny bog frogs
Hopping through the stones
Black wet turf
Standing in a rick
Happy to be here
As I look from the bog
At the fog across the mountain.

Eibhlís Ní Fhearchaillaigh

The Blue

Off the edge and into the blue
Feeling a thing that is beautifully true
Sinking deeper, there's not a sound,
There's a terrible weight, but there's nothing around

I look up and I can't see it well
I know it's there but there's no feel or smell
I can lie on a silky floor
I can feel as though I can soar

I feel a strain as I pull myself up
I hope that again I will have the luck
To feel that something that is so true
As leaping into an undiscovered blue.

Sarah Robb

By the Sands

White crusted waves fringe the sandy beach
Rounded pebbles are sifted through the sea's fingers
The wood from a shipwreck is spewed from the wave's mouth
From the depths of the sea comes a chorus of gurgles

As the sun rises over the land
The first rays fall on the deep blue surf
The sea giggles as her cold depths are warmed
As a new day arises, new life is brought to the shore

The beach is sacred stillness
Set apart from every other place
Nowhere can compare with the sandy shore
As the early morning sunlight glints off the waves.

Gemma Pudney

Ice

Icicles hanging from wet clothes
Cold wind biting at my toes
Eyes watering and a cherry nose.

Jade Turner

Ice

Icicles are frozen drips of water
Cold and transparent they hang from our roofs
Everlasting until the sun comes out.

Eibhlís Ní Fhearchaillaigh

The Sea

A warm summer's day
I lie upon the sand
I hear the screams of children
Playing on the sand

I see the children playing
So free on the shore
I feel so trapped
I can't come here anymore

As I slip back in
I'm cold and the sun doesn't burn
And I leave this warm peaceful shore
Never to return.

Andrew Hobbs

Ocean

The ocean pours water everywhere
It brings water upon new shores
The tide sweeps the water against the cliffs
The ocean is like a sunless strand near the reefs

The ocean is a golden bay of fish and shells
That stretches far and wide
In this golden bay the seaweed sways
To and fro in a sparkling dance

When the ocean lays to rest
And when the moon sets the stars alight
The dreary wind pushes the water
Against the cliffs again
But after that the water hushes
The only sound is the ocean whimpering
And the waves journeying blind.

Charlotte Mahé

La Tempête

La tempête se réveille
En criant dans nos oreilles

La tempête fait rage
Un peu comme un orage

La tempête nous pousse
Comme une balle en mousse

La tempête nous fait peur
Elle nous bloque à l'intérieur

La tempête va de ville en ville
Comme dans un parcourt de billes

La tempête fait des dégâts
Partout où elle va.

Sarah Pearson

The Wind

The wind is cold
The wind is breezy
The wind can sometimes make you wheezy

The wind is here
The wind is there
The wind is almost everywhere

It can be chilly
It can be mild
It can make your hair go wild

It can be soft
It can be loud
It can blow away any cloud

I like the wind
I like its puff
But when it's stormy
I've had enough!

Hannah Dimond

Lightning

Lights up the sky
It cracks and strikes the trees
Gold it is shaded with a touch of yellow
Haunting my mind with fear
Twinkles and flashes like the stars
Night is when it strikes
Igniting the sky
Nervous
Glitters in the dark night sky.

Breffney Cogan

Why was I not Told?

The flowers are all growing
But I'm getting wet
The grass and trees are all getting a drink
But I'm getting wet
All the umbrellas are turned up
But all I have is my leaky hood
And I'm getting wet
Why was I not told it would rain?

David Mouraud

Les Tornades

Tout en volant
Les tornades
Boivent de la limonade
Pour répandre leurs grenades
Sous les toits des marchands
Et là c'est la pagaille
Nos tympans font aïe!
Et les tornades font pan-pan!
Une partie du monde a mal.

Damien Trochu

La Marée Noire

La mer était cool
Jusqu'à ce que l'Erika coulât
Elle avançait lentement
Lentement, lentement…

Un jour elle toucha les côtes
Mais ce n'était pas de notre faute
Des bénévoles nettoyaient les plages
Les rochers, mais elle revenait sur le sable

Elle polluait tout mais tout
Sur le sable il y avait plein de boue
Tellement de boue qu'ils n'osaient
Pas venir aider à nettoyer.

Zita McCarthy

It's Raining

It's raining cats and dogs
The dog is barking
While the chestnut leaves fall
The tomcats scattering for shelter
The leaves remaining on the tree
Are dripping and dropping
The noises of my rain jacket
Mix in with the other orchestral sounds
I can feel the atmosphere changing
The sun is beaming
Through the branches.

Colm Ó'Drisceoil

Leaves

Leaves are falling
Leaves are scattering
And blowing in the sky
All the colours on the ground
A sight for passers-by
But winter comes
The trees are bare
And all the colours aren't there.

Shannen McKeegan

Far Away

Twinkle, twinkle, star in the sky
Why are you up there so high?
I would like to go and see
If you are big or small like me.

Dawn Thompson

The Tree

I wish I were a tree
Because then I could see
All the people below me
And far out to sea.

A Magic Garden

Sharon Ruane

The Monster I Met

The monster I met
Has huge front teeth
He has fourteen arms
And seventeen feet

He has twenty-five eyes
And a huge floppy ear
And one look at him
Will make you shiver with fear

For he has twenty-two heads
And sixty-three toes
With large purple bits
Hanging out of his nose

He came from Mars
In a very large shoe
And quickly he said,
'I want to eat you'.

So there was a great chase
But he soon caught me
He smiled and said,
'I'll have you for tea'.

But in the end
It wasn't a sin
I saved the world
Because I ate him.

Rebecca Noonan

The Alien Hair Grabber

Sid is me pal
Me pal is Sid
The thing 'bout Sid is this -
Sid's an alien
Sure as can be
He's also a hair grabber
He took me to
his laboratory
sat me on a chair and
boom! Gone was me hair
Me hair was gone
But we're still great pals
Sid and me.

Andrea McGoey

Our Journey

We often stop here
the sights to see
But that's a secret
between you and me.

We need some rest
before we go home
If someone comes
we stay still as gnomes.

I am tall
where will I go?
Little horsey
can stoop so low.

Travelling all day
in cold and wet
Little horse eager
to reach home I bet.

Why are we stopping here today?
No place for horses,
no oats, no hay.

Soon we move onwards
homeward bound
Not forgetting
the beauty, the stillness
all around.

Kevin Collins

The Magic Garden

When I opened my back door
I was in a magic garden
Where the cat was dead
The trees were playing chess
And the grass was having a party
Then I went home
It was the best ten seconds of my life.

Jessica Mullins

Venus

Venus walked away out of space
Because one day it grew legs
It floated for a while to find where it could go
But it didn't have eyes
So it bumped into Earth and into Mars
While walking on its way
It met the Milky Way
They became great friends
And that is how my poem ends.

Kathrin Elskemper

Ene Mene

Ene mene
ming mang
kling klang
ose pose packe dich
eia weia weg.

Conor Higgins

Humpty Dumpty

Humpty Dumpty was an egg
Humpty Dumpty had one leg
How did he walk?

Noora Hannula & Nadia Kähkönen

Muumio

Urheat retkeilijät pyramidissa kulkee
Mutta Muumion kirous heidät sisälle sulkee

Urhein retkeilijöistä oven väliin kuolee
Muut surunkaiverruksen seinään vuolee

Tunnelissa vaeltavat
Ja ansat laukeavat

Heidän äänensä hukkuvat tuuleen
Pysähtyvät eteen oven suuren

Näkivät loven
Joka avasi oven

'Nyt kaivetaan multaa
niin löydetään kultaa'

Jotain oli kaiverrettu rautaan
Mutta se jää ikuiseksi salaisuudeksi
Muumion hautaan.

Joe Hughes

Clematis Faction

A strange plant crept into the garden shed
Uninvited - to prepare for bed
It wrapped itself around the spoke of my bike
And gave my sister a terrible fright

Of the cramped conditions
Not many lived to tell the tale
Lawnmower, tools, strimmer
Garden furniture nor pail

Then the green menace, from outside the place,
Crawled further into the limited space
All along the back wall, down onto the floor
Up the other side and then clung to the door

Dad's quite sentimental
About things that grow
It's a living species
Don't you know

While mum was outraged
And prepared for action
Ready to execute
The green-eyed faction

Postponing the inevitable
Until the following day
She was astounded to find a beautiful plant
With flowers and petals
So decided to let the clematis settle.

Maitiú MacArdáil

The Onion Head

I met a man
With an onion-shaped head
It seemed to rise to a point
Layers and layers around his ears
Big red eyes, full of tears.

He cried a lot
But then so would you
With onion skin
And features too -
Eyes and ears, nose and mouth
All made of onion
From the inside out!

Andrew Waugh

The Multifever

The multifever's in Storyland today
First was Goldilocks
With chickenpox
Frogs and snails
With puppy dogs' tails
Mammy Bear has porridgitis
Wicked Witch has warts
Little Jack Horner sat in a corner
With a thumb stuck in a pie
Hickory, dickory, dock
The mouse fell off the clock
Jack Sprat ate all the tarts and
His wife drank all the beer
This is what the Multifever did
I think it's very queer.

James O'Mahony

Superboy

My name is Superboy
I have super powers
I eat for hours.

I'm really, really long
And very, very strong.

I chase Supergirls
With long, yellow curls.

Andrew Duignan

I had a Dream

I had a dream last night
in bed
that I fell down the stairs
and bumped my head

I saw the moon
I even saw Mars
but the thing that amazed me
was the stars

I flew through space
with a little green man
who brought me to the place
where time began

The trek through space
was ever so cool
till mam came in and
woke me for school.

Moll Linehan

Venus Sneezed

When Venus sneezed
It was havoc
It was such a commotion
Everyone was blown out of their beds
The day Venus sneezed
It was worse than a hurricane
It was over force 143
The wind was incredible
The day Venus sneezed.

My Throat

One day my throat was sore
So I went to the doctor at half-past four
He told me my throat was so bad
My legs had to suffer because he was mad
So I went to the hospital fearing the worst.

Camille Duval

Papa Passe la Paille

Papa passe la paille a papi
Papi n'ose pas plier la paille
Il pose la paille sur la pile
Le papillon se pose pile sur la paille.

Raphael Buttigieg

The Silly Family

The Silly family consisted of six
never-ending mixed-up things
The father used to fall
off the wall
The mother hung the clothes
with her toes
The twins used to drink
mugs full of ink
The little fat girl
had only one curl
The grandfather was always snoring
when the rain was pouring.

RUTH VAUGHAN

Hippopotemela

Do you remember Africa, Molly?
And our feet in the river muck
Where we wallowed and swallowed
As we hoped we weren't followed
Down the low-lying lane
Where we soothed our pain
In the mud that went splud
As we listened to the thud
Of the great big oof! behind me
You know,
The one that broke my knee
As he stood on me
And gave me a flea
That bit my poor little bottom
That gave me a bump
That looked like a lump
And made me fall with a thump
And when everybody laughed
I acted like a grump

Never more Molly never more
The mud may go splud
But we won't hear the thud
'Cause we'll be in...
New York!

Joe Hughes

Alienation

Now boy
Don't play the fool
Tell me why you are late for school

Well Sir...you see...Aliens invaded!!
They gave me a fright
I'm sure it'll be on the news tonight

They pulled me into a spaceship
Don't ask me why
And flew away into the sky

After a while
They beamed me down
But I landed fifteen miles out of town

I walked straight here
And you ask me to explain!
I'm going through psychological pain!

So boy,
That's your explanation
I'm sure that's just your mind's creation

Tell me God
Why is life so cruel
I mean 500 lines for being late for school!

Wouter Ekelaar

De UFO

Rustig zweeft hij door het heelal
Maar dan opeens een harde knal...
O nee, een ruimtekwal!
Zijn tentakels zijn dik
En zijn hoofd is smal.
Ik vuur een laser af
Recht op zijn hoofd
hij laat me los
Want hij is verdoofd
Een fotonraket...BAM!
Hij spat uit elkaar
Zijn tentakels
Vliegen in het rond
En ik schrik me naar.

Labhrás Ó'Conchúir

One Bright Morning

One bright morning
In the middle of the day
Two sleeping boys
Came out to play
Sitting down
They both stood up
One said, 'hello'
The other, 'good luck'
One pulled an axe
And shot my foot
The other drew a gun
And sliced my bum
With both eyes shut
They looked around
Then jumped up high
On the ground.

ORLA THOMPSON

The Silvery Woods

Whose woods these are I just don't care
And stopping now, it isn't fair
For my horse is tired and weak
Now it's not fair to blame it all on my horse
For I myself am so meek.

A chitter chatter of the teeth
A sniffle of the nose
Hear the gallop of my horse's feet
Can't even smell a rose.

All the trees are silvery white
As we ride through the night
The only thing to guide us
Is my little lantern light.

Christine O'Mahony

Father Time

I have seen the mountains rise,
Since the discoveries of the wise.

I have seen the birth of man,
I have been here since life began.

I am rusting, though never corroded,
I am passing, though never gone.

I can be spent, though never paid out,
I can be saved, though never passed on.

I have seen the rise of majesties,
I have seen the fall of dynasties.

I have been here for many a year,
Yes, I have seen it all my dear.

Jerl Norden

Headus

Kord istus pilvepiiril seal
Headus pilvetupsu peal
Ja lugupilli mängis see pillike seal

Teise pilvetupsu peal
Istus vanakurat seal
Ühe lillekese peal.

Ewen Qellec

L'Ange et le Citron

L'orange a un goût d'ange
Le python a un goût de citron
En mélangeant ces deux parfums
On obtient un parfum d'angecitron
Un jour l'homme prit ce parfum
Ce parfum d'angecitron
Il le mit dans un flacon
Et le vendit à très bon prix.

Niamh Jordan

My Balloon

I have a little yellow balloon
It shines so brightly
It's like the moon

My balloon has stars painted on
That sparkle like
The sea by night

When my balloon
Floats up high
I'm carrying around
My very own sky.

The Leaves Are Turning

Deborah Donnelly

Seasons

I know it's summer
not by the sun
or flowers
or birds that sing
but by the long days.

I know it's autumn
not by the brown of the leaves
or bare trees
but by the conker fights on the roads
and yards full of children playing in the leaves.

I know it's winter
not by the grey skies
or dark nights
or snow falling
but by the snow fights outside.

I know it's spring
not by the lambs
or things blossoming from roots to leaves
but by the daisy, and
roses bright red.

Niall Ó'Dulacháin

Autumn

Summer days are over
Autumn is on its way
Soon leaves will fall
And scatter all away

I do not like the autumn
It doesn't seem to be
Very cold or very warm
Sandwiched in it seems to me.

Aileen O'Mahony

Autumn

Autumn is the season I like best,
Into warmer clothes I get dressed.
With the leaves I make a big pile,
When I'm finished I have a big smile.
I call my friends,
And we leap,
Into the great big colourful heap!

Carly McClenaghan

Autumn Time

It's nearly autumn once again
The leaves are turning
from green to red, then golden crisp
In the lane the children
are running through the leaves
rustling through the night
In the woods the trees are bare
With nothing on them only their bark
When you look out you can
feel the lovely breezy wind
on your face
Then you awake
You look outside
You can't see the leaves
They have disappeared
Autumn time is over.

Shane Redmond

Autumn

Autumn leaves of brown, gold and red
Swirl and float around my head
Farmers harvest fruit and veg
While the gardener prunes and trims his hedge
Swallows return from their annual vacation
And build a new home in a sheltered location
Squirrels are busy storing their nuts
To share with their families
For the long winter months.

Andrew Hobbs

Winter

When the icy breeze freezes
the lake
Winter begins.
The blanket
of snow covers the
barren ground
Smothering every stone
and twig.

The icy wind sweeps
the desolate trees
The footprints of humans
hidden by a frost
of icy flakes.

The day grows darker
The moon comes out
and lights the
night sky
The icicle sparkles
in the moonlight.

Heloïse Moune

L'Hiver

L'hiver est déjà là,
Il fait très froid
Mais on est bien au chaud,
Devant le fourneau.

Déjà, la neige tombe,
Et les flocons inondent
De blanc le paysage
Et ils fouettent ton visage.

Les gens décorent leurs maisons
Et tricotent avec de la laine de mouton
De beaux pulls.
Les enfants dans leur bain
Font des bulles
Et ornent les sapins
De lumière.

Et les petits chats
Qui errent
Dans le froid.

L'homme est parfois cruel.
Les animaux en ont marre de leurs duels.

Aidin Hegarty

Winter

Outside it is snowing
The wind is blowing
Children out at play
In the garden
All the day
They sing
They play
Till day
Goes away.

Conchúr Ó'Tréinfhir

A Winter's Morn

Snow falls
Snowballs
I'm lying in bed
Duvet to my head
Wind blows
Mildness goes
I'm tucked up neatly
I am sleepy.

Jonathan Morrow

Awakening

Flowers sleeping under the snow
Awakening when the spring winds blow
Leafless trees so bare before
Sprouting plump green shoots once more
Snowdrops, daffodils and crocuses
Brighten any dull and barren floor
Spring lambs running and jumping with glee
Hedgehogs, badgers and young foxes born to be free
This is a time for a spring in our step
Joy in our hearts, no more to regret.

Shane O'Sullivan

Spring

The bees are getting honey
The Queen is not doing a thing
But that's all part of spring
All the children shouting and ready to leap
And the animals waking from
Their long winter sleep
The daffodil buds are opening
But that's all part of spring.

The flowers are starting to grow
The grass needs a mow
The gardening shops are busy
The cash register goes chi-ching!
But that's all part of spring.

All the flower buds are shooting
The colours of spring come out
Everyone wants to shout
The birds spread their wings
But that's all part of spring.

Kate Murphy

Spring

Flowers are blooming
Trees are grooming
Buds are sprouting
Children shouting
Bulbs shooting
Owls hooting
Spring is here today
Animals are coming
And I am running
My brother's screaming
Because the grass is gleaming
Spring is here today.

Celebrate

Maitiú MacArdáil

Easter

Easter egg paper shiny and bright
Making children squeal with delight
Easter bunnies hopping by
Will we catch one, let us try

Easter lambs jumping to and fro
Easter flowers beginning to grow
April showers every day
Tell us spring is on the way!

Shane Redmond

Hallowe'en

I peer outside – there's something there
There's something there that spikes my hair
I know it's Hallowe'en

Witches, witches
With their grins
And pointy hats and pointy chins
They know it's Hallowe'en

Gremlins, goblins,
Skip and leap
With ugly faces
They're ready to reap
They love Hallowe'en

The Devil,
With skin of fiery red
Haunting spirits of the dead
With horns sprouting from his head
Scary, scary, Hallowe'en.

Jim O'Hagan

Hallowe'en Pie

A frog's foot
A lizard's toe
A squishy eyeball
For my foe

A little skull
And a big thigh
Yum, yum, yum
My Hallowe'en pie.

JEAN-PIERRE PACE

The Life of Witches

Black witches fly through the sky
Over land and over sea
Why and where are they going?
Nobody dare ask
Witches feed on black slimy snakes
And drink green jelly slime
They sleep up high on the dark black clouds
So no one can get them or steal their fine broom
Their black cats howl through the night
As they watch the witches in flight.

Diarmaid De Bhál

An Sciathán Leathair

Suas síos
Suas síos
Ó thaobh go taobh
Ag usáid a radar
Tá macalla i ngach slí
Ní feidir lei éalú
Ó sheomra an tí

Ag screadáil sa dorchadas
Ní thuigeann sí go bhfuil
An éalú amach an doras
Tá fathach le folt ghruaige
Chun í a scuabadh

Tá sé an-gharbh
Sin an fáth go bhfuil sí
Nach mór marbh
Ní maith lei an áit seo
Tá sé cosúil le h-Ifreann
Ní thuigeann sí go bhfuil
An éalú amach an doras.

Daniel Manning

The Haunted Woods

Down in the haunted woods
A ghostly figure stood
They say his eyes were green
But yet no one has seen

We didn't dare to venture there
Although sometimes we tried
To take a glimpse or even see
If this creature was alive

Then one night at Hallowe'en
When everyone was brave
Down to the haunted woods we went
And came upon a grave

Up jumped a ghostly figure
His eyes they shone so bright
We did not hang around to see
We were so frightened by the sight.

CLAUDIO CARUANA

Walking Alone in the Dark

I hate walking alone in the dark
It is a little bit creepy
Spooky noises all around
Leaves rustling
Are sighs of ghosts
My spooky shadow
Is someone following me?
Trees bending down
Ready to grab me
Cats mewing all night long
Like babies abandoned in the dark.

Christine O'Mahony

Hallowe'en

Hallowe'en night
Time when mortals
Start to panic.

Time of magic,
Time of omens,
Time when witches
Gather in covens.

Time of demons,
Time of portents,
Time of panic,
Time of potions.

Witches fly
Skeletons clatter
Goblins creep
Windowpanes shatter.

Trick or treating
The dead awake
Shadowy beings
Shift and shake.

Lanterns glow
With an eerie light
Watch out!
Beware!
It's Hallowe'en night!

Gerard Black

Haunted House

As the doors creak
And the wind blows
As the windows shatter
And dogs howl
The flicker of a lantern
Is the only light
As you walk forward
Your footsteps echoing and echoing
You dare not take another step
But must
Suddenly the opening of a door
Beside you
You drop the lantern and
Run for your life
You cannot go back
It must stay.

Jane Quinn

The Ghost

Last Hallowe'en night
I went to bed
I heard a noise
And covered my head

I took down the sheet
To take a look
And suddenly, got hit by a book
There was a shadow on my wall
Standing at least six feet tall

He was as white as white could be
His big beady eyes kept staring at me
I got such a fright
I turned on the light
And then the ghost
Went out of sight.

Aimée Auchincloss

A Scare

What is it walking outside in the dark?
Is it a ghost? Oh, poor Mr Park
Who lives all alone with rats
Even though he prefers cats

What is it tapping at the window so gently?
Is it a ghost? Oh, poor Mr Bentley
Who almost fell off a cliff when no one was near
Cover your ears and pretend you can't hear

What is it dripping downstairs in the kitchen?
Is it a ghost? Oh, poor Mr Ditchen
Who drowns with his dog in the cold grey stream
Cover your eyes and pretend it's a dream.

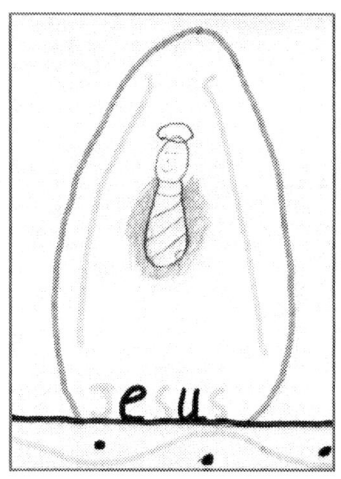

Ailbhe Cashman

Christmas Time

The Christmas tree
Presents for me
The North Star
A stable so far
The sunlight does go
Then comes the snow
'Tis a time of peace
All wars shall cease
'Tis a time of love
Because Santa comes
We get dolls, books and toys
Action men for boys
The trees with lights
The starry nights
The turkey, the ham
And sometimes the lamb
For Christmas is a time to remember
The joy of a long ago December.

ANNIINA KOSKINEN

A Christmas Eve

I wake up early in the morning
I'll wake up mother and father too.
We shall go singing in the church
I'll get the Christmas spirit from it.

During the daytime
we'll go to the city
to look in the Christmas windows.

In the evening
we'll eat the Christmas meal
good, tasty, plentiful.

Then I'll decorate the Christmas tree
and I'll open all the Christmas gifts.

And finally, I'll go to bed.

Lianne Ní Chárthaigh

Oíche Nollag

Oíche Nollag a bhí ann
Is bhí na páistí ag masiú an crann
Hip! Hip! Hurae!
Tá Daidí na Nollag ag teacht
Go dtí mo thigh
Agus tabhairfaidh sé mo bhronntanas dom
Agus nuair a íosfaidh sé an bia d'éarfaidh sé
Yum! Yum!

Tá gach duine ina gcodladh go sámh
Agus tá Daidí na Nollag
Ina leaba
Tá gliondar air
Tá a chroí ag preabadh
Anois is feidir leis dul a chodladh.

Katriina Hallama & Onerva Heikka

Joulukuusi

Olipa kerran joulukuusi, joka hussi:
'Lempiruokani on perunamuusi!'
Tuli metsään silloin saha
tosi kauhea ja paha
Se kuusen vei
ja kuusi sanoi metsälle: 'Hei!'

Ihmisten ilmoille kuusi vietiin
ja siellä se sitten koristeltiin
'On juurellani lahjoja
nuo ihmiset ovat kyllä ihan kahjoja'
sanoi kuusi jonka lempiruoka oli perunamuusi.

Colm Ó'Drisceoil

Fireworks

Fireworks whizz and swizz in the air
With fireworks your sky won't be bare
They crackle and glide on their way
Then they disappear and fade away
But the next night, they'll go up
All through the sky
And please stay back
If you don't want to die.

Jane Moriarty

The Special Star

I was an ordinary star
The smallest of my lot
But I was quite content
Being rooted to the spot

One night I heard a message
A voice from up above
I had to see the little King
Who'd fill the world with love

At first I was very frightened
But my brothers urged me on
I set off with a happy heart
My journey had begun

I sped past gulfs and deserts
Over fountain, hill and glen
I was followed by three strangers
Who were really three wise men

At last I came to Bethlehem
The sight was one to see
A Saviour in a manger
Smiling kindly up at me

Some shepherds stood there, praising
They had lambs to give the King
While angels above the stable
Continued to sweetly sing

I'm still here to this day
Thinking of the first Noel
I look on in joyful memory
And hear the Christmas bell.

Anaïs Tuco

L'An 2000

L'an 2000 c'est facile, un 2 et trois 0
Ça fera bien 2000 et on aura l'euro
Des pays sont en guerre
Pendant que le président fait ses bonnes manières
Les papillons s'accoupleront
Et nous les aimerons
Les filles, les femmes seront belles
Les coccinelles ressembleront aux hirondelles
Nous serons moins malades grâce aux médicaments
Et nous pourrons avoir plus d'argent
Nous irons dans les magasins
Acheter des jouets avec nos copains
Nous irons voir les enfants handicapés
Pour qu'ils viennent jouer.

Brian Heappey

Midnight 2000

The millennium bells are ringing
They welcome in the year
And fill our hearts with gladness
With hope and joy and cheer

Celebrate 2000
The world erupts in praise
From Tonga to New York
The skies are set ablaze

Bring in the new millennium
With hopes for lasting peace
And pray to God that finally
All terror and war will cease.

MARIE BELLUGUE

Pour l'An 2000

Les enfants de l'an 2000
Que deviendront-ils?

Tempête et marée noire
Auront-ils toujours espoir?

Kosovo, Tchetchénie
Que eur réserve la vie?

Chômage et pauvreté
Seront-ils épargnés?

L'amour et l'amitié
Sauveront l'humanité!

Haili-Michaël

A l'An 2000

Je voudrais qu'il n'y ait plus de racisme
Je voudrais qu'il n'y ait plus de victimes dans les séismes

J'espère qu'il n'y aura plus de maladie
Que sourira la belle vie

Que les animaux vivent toujours en troupeau
Et qu'ils vivent près de l'eau

Qu'il n'y ait plus de guerre
Et que la paix règne sur terre.

VANESSA MEADE

Millennium Feelings

Millennium feelings in the air
Candles and parties everywhere
2000 years have now gone by
Joy and laughter filling the earth and sky

Millennium feelings in our hearts
Thinking of people far apart
Cards being sent to family and friends
Hoping the happiness never ends

Millennium feelings in our home
Thinking of people lonely and alone
You light your candle and say your prayer
Thanking God for always being there.

Nine Innings

Mark Camilleri

In the Park

The sun shines like a huge torch
Children run and scream
Their laughter like hyenas
Babies wail and cry
Like screeching, grinding brakes
Children swinging on the bars
Like monkeys on jungle trees
The slide with its long neck
Like a huge grazing brontosaurus
Brown bins all around
Remind me of monsters' mouths
I see lots of fragrant flowers
Like colourful stars in the beautiful sky
I say to myself
How wonderful it is
How much greater must our blessed
Creator be!

Teerapong Dabreteau

La Musique

Pas de panique!
Il y a de la musique
Pour que les moustiques
Avec leur dard piquent
C'est bien quand on fait de la musique
On peut aller en pique-nique
Voilà une brique qui fait des bruits: des «CRICS!»
Les crics
De la voiture n'arrêtent jamais de faire des pics
Dans les bars, il y a des alcooliques
Qui vont au cirque
Tellement ils ont trop bu, ils titubent, «HIC!»
C'est pathétique!

Linda Kelly

Tooth Fairy

The tooth fairy is a friend of mine
She creeps into my room at half-past nine
She lifts my pillow as I am asleep
I dare not open my eyes to peep
She takes my tooth without a sound
But oh, next morning I find a shiny pound.

James O'Mahony

Teacher Fell into the Pool

Our class was having an ordinary
Day at the pool.
The teacher sat on a stool.
The stool rocked and knocked
Our teacher right into the pool.
We all got such a fright
To see such a sight
To see a poor teacher like that.
The teacher said no more
She just walked out the door.

Arthur Templé

C'est Bien

C'est bien pour certains
Ou pas pour les autres
Ça donne mal au ventre
Aussi aux intestins

C'est vraiment bizarre
Oh oui ça c'est vrai
La super boisson
A couleur marron.

Cindy Garda

La Maîtresse

Répétons sans cesse:
Vive la maîtresse!
Nous l'aimons beaucoup
Car elle apprend tout
A chanter, à lire
A compter, à écrire
A l'école on est joyeux
A l'école on est heureux!
Répétons sans cesse:
Vive la maîtresse!
Mon poème est fini
Et c'est tout pour aujourd'hui.

Patrick Cronin

Mammy

Mammy's too ill today
To take me outside to play
So I'll stroke her head
While she lies in bed
And smooth her headache away.

Ailbhe Cashman

The Beach

Sandcastles on the shore
Ruins of those that are no more
Children screaming
Adults dreaming
Fast motorskis
Buzzing about the seas
Seagulls screeching
Lifesavers teaching
Catching the sun
Having some fun
Kids in their togs
Waterlogged dogs
Boys pulling hair
Dads on the chair
But alone on the cliff
Stood a forlorn figure
Curled up crying
Like it was dying
This figure could only be me
Crying out for my cut knee.

Arnaud le Cadre

Pourquoi?

Pourquoi les litières miaulent-elles?
Pourquoi les arbres chantent-ils?
Pourquoi la maison parle-t-elle?
Pourquoi les lits ronflent-ils?

JEAN-PIERRE PACE

A Street Full of Noisy Traffic

As I sat in Russell Square
I watched the traffic pass
All the traffic zoomed
To the next set of traffic lights
That blink like Christmas sights
When the traffic stops
People cross the zebra crossing
Like a flock of sheep in danger
Horns hooting, brakes grinding
Motorbikes screeching
Ambulances and police cars wailing
Oh! What a lot of noise and hurry
It is good to sit back
And not to be part of it.

Taru Takamaa

Suomi

Suomi on meidän rakas kotimaamme
sen me eläinten kanssa jaamme.
Talvella maahan sataa paljon lunta
tuntuu kuin se olisi ihanaa unta.
Keväällä voi korvaläpät pois heittää
ruohomatto jo maan peittää.
Kohta tulee lämmin kesä
linnunpoikasia on täynnä pesä.
Syksyllä lehdet puista putoo
äiti villapaitoja lapsille kutoo.
Suomi onkin mukava maa
täällä metsissä vapaasti juoksennella saa.

Clodagh Hogan

Little Boys should be Seen and Not Heard

If the weather is fine
Little boys will run about
They will jump up and down
And scream and shout

They will pretend to be good
So you will give them a sweet:
'I never make noise and
I always wash my teeth.'

They want lots of toys
Like toy cars and guns
They want lots of sweets
Like cakes and buns

Behind those little smiles
They are wild and crazy
Behind those twinkling eyes
They are stubborn and lazy

Little boys squeak and squawk
Like a bird
And that's why little boys
Should be seen and not heard.

STEPHEN FIELD

Soccer

I like playing soccer
We play it in school
I play in mid-field
I can cross the ball into the goal

I went by train to Dublin
To play a football final
Our team played well
But lost by one goal

Every Wednesday we play
Football with our teachers
Sometimes we play matches
The referee is a woman
She is very good, bad
Angry and blows her whistle.

EDWARD O'ROURKE

Spiderman

Spiderman is Peter Parker
He has a girlfriend
Mary Jane
He can fire out webs
From his hand
And he can climb walls

Doctor Octopus, Goblin
And Venom
Are his enemies
Octopus makes crazy inventions
With bad intentions

Venom's webs are sticky
His traps are often tricky
Goblin has a hoverboard
Shaped as a bat
And he fires out
Pumpkin bombs

When Spiderman's
Web cartridges run out
Something always saves
Him
Catgirl always looks out
To save him.

Catherine Hayes

I Don't Mind

I have a grandfather called Billa
He dresses in women's clothes
In case this goes any further
I think everybody should know

Each year he does panto
At the Cork Opera House
He sings and tells stories
And makes people laugh

He dances with the small children
And has a heart of gold
Everyone starts to clap
As he tells each joke.

Doireann Ní Ghráinne

A Visit to the Doctor

I went into the office
The doctor said straight through
I was so afraid of the doctor
My face had gone bright blue

I walked down the corridor
And looked in through the door
I saw a little girl shouting out,
'Please, please, no more.'

I opened my mouth to scream
But nothing would come out
My mum said, 'Hurry up, or
The doctor will give out.'

I walked into the dreaded room
The doctor said, 'Sit down.'
I walked towards the chair
And he looked at me with a frown

First he checked my temperature
Then he checked my arm
And after all this time
It was just a false alarm!

Sophie Kearney

The Playground

The playground in our school is behind a wall
You can't see in unless you are tall
Our playground when it rains is full of muck
So you have to be careful or your shoes will get stuck
Our playground has little beds of flowers
But no little shelter in case of showers
We go to the playground to talk and have fun
But there's no room to have a good run
Our playground does not have slides or swings
Or any of children's favourite things
But when you are happy with your friend
You wish playtime never ends.

Nadia Kähkönen

Suomen Luonto

Kuusi nuokkuu tuulessa
Metsässä suuressa
Kyllä kohta iloita saan:
Kun valkoinen lumi peittää Suomen maan

Kuulen huminan kaislojen
Suomi on maa järvien

Mitä parempaa voi toivoakkaan
Kun rikkaus tämä Suomen maan?

Servane Warot

Poème

Je veux faire un poème
pour que tout le monde l'aime.

Je pourrais faire un poème qui se passe sous les cocotiers
ou sous les palmiers,
avec une serviette de plage sur le rivage.

Mais pas sur un coin ensoleillé,
je ne veux pas retourner chez moi brûlée.

Ou un poème qui se passe à Nantes
Cette ville rassurante et attirante.

En se promenant dans les rues,
on voit un boucher
qui a un client qui se plaint que sa viande n'est pas hachée.

On voit aussi un Portugais qui parle
avec un employé d'un restaurant japonais,
un policier qui inflige une amende à une marchande
et un Quimpérois vendre des petits pois.

Mais en fait, ce poème
Je l'ai trouvé
Il est même écrit sur ce papier.

Assia Khetib

De Toekomst

Wat zou er in de toekomst zijn?
Auto's die in de ruimte zweven?
Of mensen die verslaffd zijn?
Als ik dat kan weten,
Zou ik dan niet meer willen leven?
Of andersom?

De toekomst is een spel
Laat hem zitten in z'n vel.

Mickaël

La Belgique

Un pays pas plus grand que la Bretagne
Plat, donc sans montagne
Séparé en trois communautés
Chacune avec ses spécialités
Moules, frites et bière
De bonnes choses pour nous satisfaire
L'accueil est chaleureux
On y vit heureux
Chic!
C'est la Belgique!

Jenny Gough

Candles

A candle is flickering
In the midst of the night
It is a strong source of heat
A giver of light

With the cold and the darkness
It puts up a great fight
It flickers and burns
With all of its might

It can also be gentle
A shy little flame
Who is frightened of the cold
And is very tame

It is unable to spread
It is very mild
It is small and weak
Like a newborn child

Some candles are strong
And powerful and wild
Not all of the time
Is a small flame mild

A flame can be dangerous
If near some things
It can jump and leap
And catch onto many things

Ancient people believed
In a kind god of all flames
Knowing the uses of candles
Should surely explain

Candles can come
In all colours, shapes and sizes
They can even bring us
Scented surprises

Candles are beautiful
Weak and strong
Some people think they are useless
But those people are wrong.

DAVID FITZGERALD

I have a Dream

To be on the Cork team
To win all medals and caps
And celebrate with the clubs

I'd like to be like Christy Ring
And score until we win
I would play at centre-back
So I could give the ball a whack

I'd take the penalties and the frees
And make the other team look like fleas

The press would adore the likes of me
And I'd 'float like a butterfly'
And 'sting like a bee'

I'd practise my hurling day and night
And I would hit the ball out of sight
In every game I'd play my best
And give the other team no rest

Some day I'll make the team
I know I will
That is my dream.

Siobhán Coady

A Dream

I have a dream to sing and dance
On stage and TV at every chance
To be on the telly and dancing around
Drinking coke because I'd be bound
To reach number one.
It would be so much fun
With make-up on and my hair in a bun
To travel the world and the seven seas
In my own private jet, a life of ease.
To dress up nicely with clothes that shimmer
With the colours of the rainbow and all the glamour
To be seen on the street giving autographs
And five minutes later to be in lots of photographs.
Using new shampoo that shines my hair
I'd think I'm worth it but I'd really care
To have a nice tan
Then I'd be flattered.
And to look real smart
But what really matters,
Is the support of my parents and friends
I would be really happy and hope it would never end.
To win an award and have an amazing smile
To be on magazines that reach for miles
Would I be really kind, sweet and nice?
If I had the choice
At the end of the day
Would I stop and stay
Just as I am?
But I am Siobhán
And I have a dream.

Aoife Corcoran

My Dream

My dream is to write many books
And have them published with beautiful covers
When people read them they'll give good looks
My books will be read by my fellow book lovers

In my books I shall also write poems
They will be funny and enjoyed by people
They won't be about fairies, witches and gnomes
Or pussycats caught up a steeple

My writings will be realistic but funny as well
Like the works of McKenna and Leach
People will chat about my books and to their friends they'll say,
"Corcoran's works are better than Dahl's 'James and the Giant Peach'"

My books will consist of poetry and prose
I shall revolve my life around writing
Everyone who's close and friendly to me knows
When I've got writer's block the tension is nail-biting

After my homework I write for ages
When I write I am really engrossed
On weekends I write pages and pages
Writing is the pastime I love the most.

Chloé Mitaine

Les Mitaines

Les mitaines
Ce sont des rennes
Du père Noël
Qui les enchaînent
Avec des chaînes
Et qui les aiment
Et qui les aiment
Et qui les aiment…

Les mitaines qu'est ce que c'est?
Ce sont des gants les mitaines.
Et les gants mitaines ce sont des gants qui
　s'arrêtent au milieu des doigts
Et voilà c'est ça des gants mitaines.
Mais ne vous inquiétez pas je suis toute entière.

ALINE ET AMANDINE

La Belgique

La Belgique
Un petit pays sympathique
Où l'on fait du bon chocolat
Mais les Bruxellois ne se vantent pas pour ça
Flamands et Wallons
Ils sont environ dix millions
Aux sons des tambours, les Gilles danseront
Et les oranges nous les rattraperons
St Nicolas, ami des enfants sages
Le six décembre descend tout droit des nuages
Et nous terminons ce poème en disant: c'est fantastique
De connaître la Belgique!

AMY NUTT

The Swing

So much depends
On that swing
To make the children
Happy everyday in spring.

Love Reigns

Rachel McDonald

The Snowman

A snowman is cold
And I mean cold
When you put your fingers in him and
Take them out again
There are some holes in him
When he starts to get hot
He starts to melt and
When he melts
You really are sad because
You really loved him and he was your
Favourite snowman and
You called him
Kenneth.

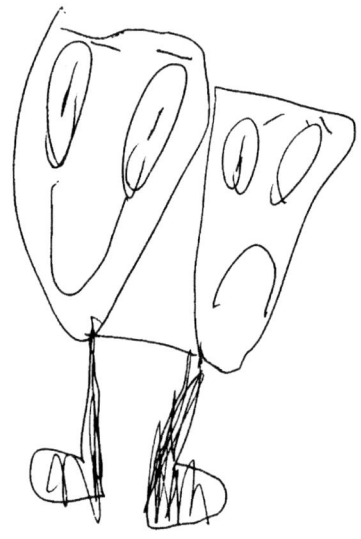

AILBHE CASHMAN

Not Gone

I may look gone
But I'm always here
My love's still strong
It grows every year
I'll still love and watch you
Always, always
As I used to.
I'll be here for more happy days
And I hope you'll love me too
As you always, always,
Used to.

Denis Murphy

Love

Love is like a turtle dove
That floats on high
In the beautiful sky

Love is like a star
A never-ending star
That twinkles in your sky
And also in your eye

Love is like a warm bath
That covers your whole body
And makes you feel
Like a special somebody

Love is looking
In your parents' eyes
And seeing the love shine back
On you and me.

James Hayes

Colm

He is eight and a half
I like him because he loves Man Utd and
I do too.
He is the best friend a boy could ever have
He is the best soccer player in the world
He is very fast at running
He comes to school everyday and
He likes it too
He has a girlfriend
He likes Barney and Friends
He likes Pokémon too
He likes Rugrats,
Chips and burgers
And he likes football too.
I like football too.

Colm Buckley

James

James is seven and a half and he is very brave
He is a very funny boy, he loves Man Utd
He is very good at soccer and very fast at running
James is the best friend ever
He is very fast at writing
He loves sums and Irish and English
He is a very holy boy
He likes Pokémon and TV and he
Likes chips and burgers and he loves
Barney and Friends
He is very good at school
He likes reading books.

Maurice Hamilton

Love Reigns

Love reigns in my heart
Everyday
My love for you
Will never go away

When you're sick
You still try your best
When you should be having
A little rest

You always try to please me
You're very unselfish it's true
My love for you
Will never die away
Mum, I love you.

Eamonn Mulholland

We are in Love

Every time I see your eyes
It makes me think of your big heart
Whenever I go on holidays
I think of you in the plane
I come home and go to your house
When you wake up I am near your bed
I am saying and you are saying
We are in love.

Ashley Henderson

Max

When I go out to play
Max comes along with me
He's black and white and very big
He's my best friend you see.

Cara Sanquest

Human Rainbow

You are the sunshine
I am your rain
I am your rainbow
To light up your day.

Mirjam Pilv

Lahkus

Lahkus toob meil ainult head
Lahkus värskendab ka pead
Ole sõpradega hea siis nad sulle
teevad head.ole lahge kõigiga
siis nad tasuvadsul pea.

Headus

Headus sulle naeru toob
Teistele ta heameelt loob
headust elus vaja ikka
et saaks eluiga pikka
Headus meile halba ei anna
siis me viha ka ei kanna
Viha kanda pole ilus
siis su heapool püsib vilus.

Sõprus

Ole sõber teistega
siis teised sõbrad sinuga
Sõprus hea on igasmõttes
ja siis on sõbrad sinu mõttes
sõpradele loota võid ja
nende poolt sa olla võid
sõpru valima ei pea ole
sõber kõigiga.

Désirée Scheer

Erinnerung

Ich hab' eine Erinnerung
zart, wie Rosenblätter
die sanft meine Wangen streicheln

Ich hab' eine Erinnerung
schön, wie die untergehende Sonne
die langsam am Horizont verschwindet.

Ich hab' eine Erinnerung
intensiv, wie die Farben
des erwachenden Frühlings

Ich hab' eine Erinnerung
Die Erinnerung an dich!

In Darkness Light

Leslie Spillane

Coffins

A dark and eerie night
A dark and eerie garden
Where stands a creepy tomb
In darkness light
A coffin
Standing alone
A creak, a step
The lid lifts open
A shadow dark and scary
A person slime and grit
He's rotting in decay
Thought that never again
Would he see the light of day
For there in his tomb,
His garden, coffin, world,
He feels death is here
And his life slowly unfurls
Before his eyes
He sees all his mysteries
The things he did
The statues he made
And his decisions
And mistakes
For now that he is dead
He regrets a lot
Of things he said
Of things he heard
Before he was doomed to rot
In his dark and eerie coffin
His dark and eerie tomb
His dark and eerie garden
He knows he is doomed.

Rebecca Noonan

Stuck

My air was running out
soon I wouldn't be able to
breathe - let alone shout
so I stopped
for a minute
remembering it all
The row with my mate
The strange old man
What was that?
A spider!
A tarantula?
A black thingy?
'My last thoughts,'
I thought.
'What will they be?'
Suddenly I heard a noise,
Footsteps?
The coffin was being prised open
'Joanne!'
My friend yelled.
'I'm so sorry,
You could have been killed.'
Everything got blurry
I think I blacked out
For all I could hear was
Yet another shout,
'Jo, don't be dead.'
My mother was there
Cradling my head.

Michael Hurley

Death

Coffin
Dead people
Ghosts
Dark
These are all the bad things of death
Worms in your eye
Playing monopoly
Death is when you're dead
Darkness falls
Decaying in your own juices
Nobody there says good-bye
In the night
Nothing but darkness.

PATRICIA PRUNTY

The Wave

Look! Look! The big wave is coming,
The words echo straight through my mind.
Without a thought I run for the hill.

It's getting closer, closer by the minute.
I will not make it, the wave is far too close.
My heart and soul will rest forever,
As I lie here under this wild but glittering sea.

My mother and brother are praying for me,
While I am here celebrating
In the land, of Tír na nÓg.

Eilis McGleur

The Wall

Twenty years now
This old wall
Still stands
Once
So beautiful
From grey to black
To white and brown
Autumn glory
The ivy gone
Life and hope
Draining away
As the end draws near
And the world begins to mourn.

SIMEON LENZ-LIPITCH

Heaven

Some day I'll go to Heaven
But not yet
Perhaps when I'm
One hundred and twenty
No sadness
No pain
But happiness
There.
Some day
I know I'll go to Heaven
But not yet.

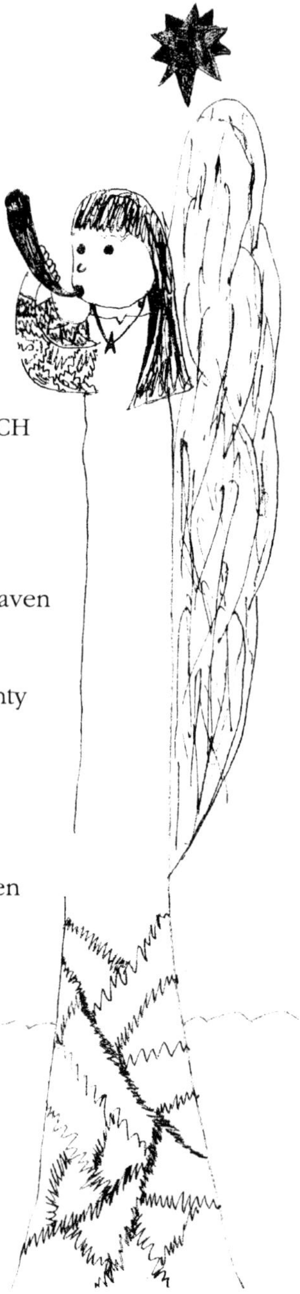

Marion Colas

Les Maladies Graves

Le cancer est une maladie grave
Il faut que ces gens-là soient braves.

D'autres maladies
Sont aussi graves que celles-ci.

D'ici quelques années
Les médecins feront des médicaments instantanés.

Ce seront des médicaments
Pour ne plus perdre ses cheveux tout le temps.

Grâce aux opérations
Il n'y aura plus de capitulation.

ASTRID COUGHLAN

There was an Old Man

There was an old man
Who lived by the sea
With no one to talk to, not even you or me
He looked through the window waiting for his love
But all he could see was a sweet gentle dove
When he got up in the morning he walked outside
Waiting for someone, that someone a bride
One day he heard a knock at the door
And when he opened it, he smiled more and more
It was his true love he longed for so long
This fantasy story has just begun
They lived together for years and years
There wasn't a cry or a sight of a tear
But one day the sea came in, one dull day
It took their sweet gentle souls away.

Jessica Lynch

Guns of Sorrow

Guns of sorrow
The shooting an ear-piercing sound
Decided they wanted a life to borrow
The sad sound that surrounds
The old lady's lamenting
It's so hard the funeral
Their friends sing
Remembering their old pals
They visit the grave
In their beloved's honour
A grave like a never-ending cave
The people who shoot their friends
Their hearts are sour.

Stephanie Fleming

The Haunting

In the graveyard shadows
The children play
Never to see another day.
Although the parents live to see
Their children are gone through catastrophe
Some in falls, some in splashes.
But there is one
Who never joins in the fun
Leaning out the gates seeking to spy
Her distraught parents passing by
She had wanted to flee
But was not set free
His finger moved, fired the gun
And that's why this child has no fun.

Jill Collins

To a Strange Place

No more abuse
No more suffering
A place with no guns
No fumes to kill

A strange light flickers before me
No longer afraid
I come out of the tunnel of darkness
My conscience has been tested
Colours of all kinds fill my head

I meet with my loved ones
We are reunited
No more pain do I suffer
No precise face do I see

I walk and see green
I see sun
I don't know where I am
But I know I'm at peace.

Sarah Bowe

Grandad

A cold damp December night
He passed away in the fading light
No tears I shed, drops of sadness I cannot find
Images of my dead grandfather flash through my mind
Images of laughter, fun and hope
My poor grandmother, I fear she will not cope
Companions for life, always side by side
The man to whom a thousand years is but a day
No wonder you hide, to your covered-in grave
I cry my final tear, no love for God in my heart
Just hatred and fear
I'm leaving now, a star shines in the east
To my most beautiful grandad: rest in peace.

Désirée Scheer

Ich Sah Sie!

Ich sah sie!
Lachend
Strahlend
Fröhlich
Jeder glaubte sie sei glücklich.
Jeder glaubte sie sei stark
Doch niemand sah ihre Angst!
Einsam und verlassen auf der Welt
Der einzge Freund
der einzge Weg
die Droge!

Ich sah sie!
Weinend
Willenlos
Hilflos
Jeder wollte ihr helfen

Jeder wollte sie befreien
Doch niemand hörte ihr zu!
Allein und vergessen auf der Welt
Der einzge Freund
der einzge Weg
der Tod!

DÉSIRÉE SCHEER

Missbraucht und Weggeworfen!

Missbraucht und weggeworfen!
Statt Liebe und Freundschaft
Hass und Tod
Sie sah nie mehr Hoffnung
nur immer die Not!

Die Freundschaft verging
die liebe verlor!
Der Hass wollte siegen
der Tod kam zuvor!

Heraus aus diesem Teufelskreis
der sich auch noch 'das leben' nennt!
Glück erfuhr sie leider nie
doch Kummer
große Qual!

Missbraucht war sie
und weggeworfen
doch sagen konnt sie's nicht
Sie heulte alles in sich rein
bis es schließlich kam!
Sie hatte Angst
die Schuld zu tagen
und sah nur einen Weg
Ader Tod war da
ihr einzger Freund
doch Erlösung fand sie nicht!

Ciara Egan

The Old Priest

The knock came to the door
Just at the midnight hour
'Father, Father,' he could hear someone roar
'Come quickly, we need you
we need you for sure.'
The old priest stuck his head out
'What is it my friend?
You're quite frightened
As if there'll soon be death.'
'Oh Father, oh Father,
'tis my brother's not well
He thinks he's dying
and that he'll go to Hell.'
'Go on,' said the priest
'I'll be there in a while.'
So he got himself ready
and got there in time
for the old man to die
With a wonderful smile.

APPENDIX

SCHOOLS INVOLVED IN
EUROCHILD 2000

Ballycroneen NS, Co. Cork:
Coady, Siobhán
Fitzgerald, David

Balscadden NS, Balbriggan, Co. Dublin:
O'Hagan, Jim
Quinn, Jane
Ruane, Sharon

Beaumont BNS, Cork:
Ó'Drisceoil, Colm

Christian Brothers College, Cork:
Hughes, Joe

Cork School Project, Cork:
Hurley, Camille
Sanquest, Cara

Creative Writing Class, Tigh Filí, Cork:
Bardon, Paul
Barry, Niamh
Collins, Kevin
Forde, Kelly
Hurley, Michael
Kelleher, Jessica
Linehan, Moll
Mullins, Jessica
Noonan, Rebecca
Paul, Lia
Spillane, Leslie

Drumachose NS, Limavady, Co. Londonderry:
Bowers, Richard
Corscadden, Ruth
Devlin, Peter
Donnelly, Deborah
Dooey, Rachel
Hemphill, Julian
Henderson, Ashley
Kirke, Robert
McAlary, Gemma
McClenaghan, Carly
McDonald, Rachel
McKeegan, Shannen
Moore, Aleisha
Morrow, Jonathan
Nutt, Amy
Pudney, Gemma
Robb, Sarah
Shiels, Laura
Thompson, Dawn
Turner, Jade

Ecole Beausoleil, La Chapelle sur Erdre, France:
Boutteau, Melanie
Garda, Cindy

Ecole de la Chauvinière, Nantes, France:
Bellugue, Marie
Colas, Marion
Haili-Michaël
Tuco, Anaïs

Ecole du Coudray, Nantes, France:
Bernard, Marion
Moune, Heloïse
Varganyi, Marion
Warot, Servane

Ecole la Cerisaie, Ste Luce sur Loire, France:
Mahé, Charlotte
Trochu, Damien

Ecole Léon-Blum, Nantes, France:
Dabreteau, Teerapong
Houël, Kristell
Qellec, Ewen
Templé, Arthur

Ecole Marcel Gouzii, Nantes, France:
Aline et Amandine
Mickaël

Ecole St Exupéry, Vigneux, France:
Duguay, Stéphanie
Duval, Camille
Dycke, Orjang
Guichard, Amélie
Lauriane, Thomas
Le Cadre, Arnaud
Mitaine, Chloé
Mouraud, David

Gemeinschaftsgrundschule, Cologne, Germany:
Elskemper, Kathrin

Gaelscoil Bheanntraí, Bantry, Co. Cork:
De Bhál, Diarmaid
Ní Chárthaigh, Lianne
Ní Fhearchaillaigh, Eibhlís
Ní Úrdail, Síle

Gaelscoil Dhún Dealgan, Co. Louth:
Jordan, Niamh
MacArdáil, Maitiú
Ní Lionnáin, Ciara
Ó'Conchúir, Labhrás
Ó'Dulacháin, Niall
Ó'Tréinfhir, Conchúr

Individual Entries:
Miller, Jayne
Ballincollig, Cork:
Lynch, Jessica
Ballydehob, Co. Cork:
Corcoran-Tadd, Athena
Corcoran-Tadd, Fionn
Galway:
Healy, Micha
Innishannon, Co. Cork:
Dagg, Benjamin
Dagg, Caitlin
Navan, Co. Meath:
Barber, Joan
McGleur, Eilis
Poynton, Karen
Pijnacker, The Netherlands:
Van der Puil, Jessica
St Luke's, Cork:
Porter, Harry

Lycée Franco-Finlandais, Helsinki, Finland:
Hallama, Katriina
Hannula, Noora
Heikka, Onerva
Kähkönen, Nadia
Takamaa, Taru

Maatulin ala-aste, Helsinki, Finland:
Koskinen, Anniina

Parcival School, Amstelveen, The Netherlands:
Ekelaar, Wouter
De Dood, Jan
Gider, Tristan
Khetib, Assia
Tol, Benjamin
Van Tongeren, Wouter

Presentation Convent NS, Bandon, Cork:
O'Mahony, Aileen
O'Mahony, Christine

Realschule Graz-Webling, Graz, Austria:
Scheer, Désirée

Rockboro NS, Cork:
Auchincloss, Aimée
Barry, Sîan
Berka, Janet
Bushe-Murphy, Billie
Broecker, Katie
Cotter, Josh
Coughlan, Astrid
Dimond, Hannah
El Sayed, Adham
Hart, Emma
Heappey, Brian
Hobbs, Andrew
Ley, Simon Anthony
McCarthy, Rebecca
McKimm, Christine
Murphy, Denis
O'Connell, Gillian
O'Neill, Julie
O'Toole, Evan
Pearson, Jonathan
Pearson, Sarah
Redmond, Shane
Sweetnam, Reggie

St Joseph's, Longford:
Cassin, Laura
Columb, Christina
Dalton, Sophie
Egan, Ciara
Gorman, Aoife
Kelly, Linda
Lawrence, Annie
Lawrence, Nancy
McGoey, Andrea
Nevin, Christine
Prunty, Patricia
Thompson, Orla

St Luke's NS, Cork:
Hogan, Clodagh
Mahony, Caoimhe

St Mary's NS, Cork:
Field, Stephen
Hayes, Catherine
O'Rourke, Edward

St Michael's NS, Arklow, Co. Wicklow:
Cashman, Ailbhe

Scoil Bhríde, Eglantine, Cork:
Collins, Jill
Corcoran, Aoife
Counihan, Emma
Fitzgerald, Aisling
Fleming, Stephanie
Gough, Jenny
Martin, Kate
McSweeney, Sheila
Moriarty, Jane
Ní Ghráinne, Doireann
O'Driscoll, Aimee
O'Dwyer, Chloe
O'Toole, Eve
Vaughan, Ruth

Scoil Bhríde, Rathdowney, Co. Laois:
Bowe, Sarah

Scoil Eoin, Innishannon, Co. Cork:
Doyle, Adrian
Murphy, Kate
O'Sullivan, Shane
Walsh, Jack

Scoil Mhuire, Cork:
Cogan, Breffney
Kearney, Sophie
McCarthy, Zita

Scoil Mhuire, Schull, Co. Cork:
Hegarty, Aidin
Lenz-Lipitch, Simeon

Scoil Phádraig Naofa, Bandon, Co. Cork:
Black, Gerard
Buckley, Colm
Hayes, James
Meade, Vanessa
O'Mahony, James
Waugh, Andrew

Scoil Phádraig NS, Strokestown, Co. Roscommon:
Duignan, Andrew
Manning, Daniel

South School, Abbeyleix, Co. Laois:
Hamilton, Maurice

Stella Maris College, Gzira, Malta:
Bartolo, Max
Buttigieg, Raphael
Camilleri, Mark
Caruana, Claudio
Cilia, Damian
Pace, Jean-Pierre

Tartu Karlova Gümnaasium, Estonia:
Norden, Jerl
Pilv, Mirjam
Courtesy of The Student Factory

Watergrasshill NS, Co. Cork:
Cronin, Patrick
Higgins, Conor
Mulholland, Eamonn
O'Mahony, Diarmuid
Savage, Cora

Youghalarra NS, Nenagh, Co. Tipperary:
Conway, Caroline
Madden, Stephanie
McKenna, Aoife